U.S. Department of
Transportation

**Federal Railroad
Administration**

Guidelines for the Specification of Blue Safety Flags in Railroad Operations

Office of Railroad
Policy and Development
Washington, DC 20590

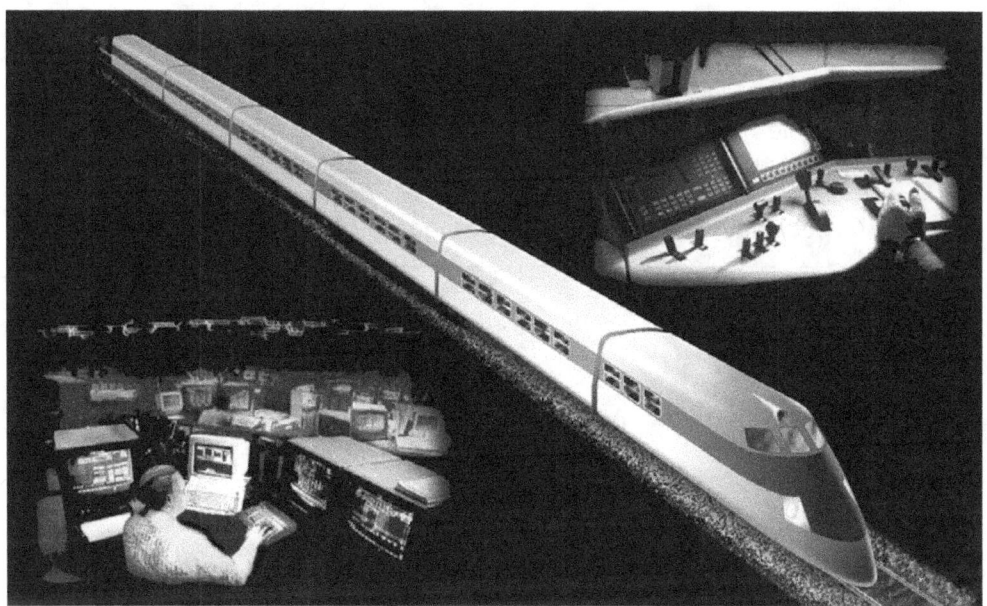

Human Factors in Railroad Operations

DOT/FRA/ORD-10/15

Final Report
December 2010

REPORT DOCUMENTATION PAGE

Form Approved
OMB No. 0704-0188

1. AGENCY USE ONLY (*LEAVE BLANK*)	2. REPORT DATE December 2010	3. REPORT TYPE AND DATES COVERED Technical Report

4. TITLE AND SUBTITLE Guidelines for the Specification of Blue Safety Flags in Railroad Operations	5. FUNDING NUMBERS RR04/FB102

6. AUTHOR(S) Daniel J. Hannon	

7. PERFORMING ORGANIZATION NAME(S) AND ADDRESS(ES) U.S. Department of Transportation Research and Innovative Technology Administration John A. Volpe National Transportation Systems Center 55 Broadway Cambridge, MA 02142	8. PERFORMING ORGANIZATION DOT-VNTSC-FRA-10-09

9. SPONSORING/MONITORING AGENCY NAME(S) AND ADDRESS(ES) U.S. Department of Transportation Federal Railroad Administration Office of Railroad Policy and Development 1200 New Jersey Avenue, SE Washington, DC 20590	10. SPONSORING/MONITORING AGENCY REPORT NUMBER DOT/FRA/ORD-10/15

11. SUPPLEMENTARY NOTES
Staff Director, Human Factors Research Program: Thomas G. Raslear, Ph.D.

12a. DISTRIBUTION/AVAILABILITY STATEMENT This document is available to the public through the FRA Web site at http://www.fra.gov.	12b. DISTRIBUTION CODE

13. ABSTRACT (Maximum 200 words)
Blue flag protection in the railroad industry provides safety to workers from the inadvertent movement of equipment on which they are working. Current Federal regulations provide minimum specifications for the devices that can be used as blue flags, allowing many devices to be used as long as they are blue. Safety standards developed by national and international committees that have been adopted throughout a wide variety of high hazard industries, however, require greater specificity in the design of safety signs and signals. An analysis of 11 commercially available blue safety flag products revealed that 5 did not meet any safety standards beyond the minimum government regulations, and only 1 met the requirements of the most stringent safety code. Recommendations are provided for blue safety flags that are consistent with the current meaning and use in the railroad industry and that meet current safety code guidelines.

14. SUBJECT TERMS Blue Flag, Railroad Safety, Color Code	15. NUMBER OF PAGES 37
	16. PRICE CODE

17. SECURITY CLASSIFICATION OF REPORT Unclassified	18. SECURITY CLASSIFICATION OF THIS PAGE Unclassified	19. SECURITY CLASSIFICATION OF ABSTRACT Unclassified	20 LIMITATION OF ABSTRACT Unclassified

METRIC/ENGLISH CONVERSION FACTORS

ENGLISH TO METRIC

LENGTH (APPROXIMATE)

1 inch (in)	=	2.5 centimeters (cm)
1 foot (ft)	=	30 centimeters (cm)
1 yard (yd)	=	0.9 meter (m)
1 mile (mi)	=	1.6 kilometers (km)

AREA (APPROXIMATE)

1 square inch (sq in, in^2)	=	6.5 square centimeters (cm^2)
1 square foot (sq ft, ft^2)	=	0.09 square meter (m^2)
1 square yard (sq yd, yd^2)	=	0.8 square meter (m^2)
1 square mile (sq mi, mi^2)	=	2.6 square kilometers (km^2)
1 acre = 0.4 hectare (he)	=	4,000 square meters (m^2)

MASS - WEIGHT (APPROXIMATE)

1 ounce (oz)	=	28 grams (gm)
1 pound (lb)	=	0.45 kilogram (kg)
1 short ton = 2,000 pounds (lb)	=	0.9 tonne (t)

VOLUME (APPROXIMATE)

1 teaspoon (tsp)	=	5 milliliters (ml)
1 tablespoon (tbsp)	=	15 milliliters (ml)
1 fluid ounce (fl oz)	=	30 milliliters (ml)
1 cup (c)	=	0.24 liter (l)
1 pint (pt)	=	0.47 liter (l)
1 quart (qt)	=	0.96 liter (l)
1 gallon (gal)	=	3.8 liters (l)
1 cubic foot (cu ft, ft^3)	=	0.03 cubic meter (m^3)
1 cubic yard (cu yd, yd^3)	=	0.76 cubic meter (m^3)

TEMPERATURE (EXACT)

$[(x-32)(5/9)]$ °F = y °C

METRIC TO ENGLISH

LENGTH (APPROXIMATE)

1 millimeter (mm)	=	0.04 inch (in)
1 centimeter (cm)	=	0.4 inch (in)
1 meter (m)	=	3.3 feet (ft)
1 meter (m)	=	1.1 yards (yd)
1 kilometer (km)	=	0.6 mile (mi)

AREA (APPROXIMATE)

1 square centimeter (cm^2)	=	0.16 square inch (sq in, in^2)
1 square meter (m^2)	=	1.2 square yards (sq yd, yd^2)
1 square kilometer (km^2)	=	0.4 square mile (sq mi, mi^2)
10,000 square meters (m^2)	=	1 hectare (ha) = 2.5 acres

MASS - WEIGHT (APPROXIMATE)

1 gram (gm)	=	0.036 ounce (oz)
1 kilogram (kg)	=	2.2 pounds (lb)
1 tonne (t)	=	1,000 kilograms (kg)
	=	1.1 short tons

VOLUME (APPROXIMATE)

1 milliliter (ml)	=	0.03 fluid ounce (fl oz)
1 liter (l)	=	2.1 pints (pt)
1 liter (l)	=	1.06 quarts (qt)
1 liter (l)	=	0.26 gallon (gal)
1 cubic meter (m^3)	=	36 cubic feet (cu ft, ft^3)
1 cubic meter (m^3)	=	1.3 cubic yards (cu yd, yd^3)

TEMPERATURE (EXACT)

$[(9/5) y + 32]$ °C = x °F

QUICK INCH - CENTIMETER LENGTH CONVERSION

QUICK FAHRENHEIT - CELSIUS TEMPERATURE CONVERSION

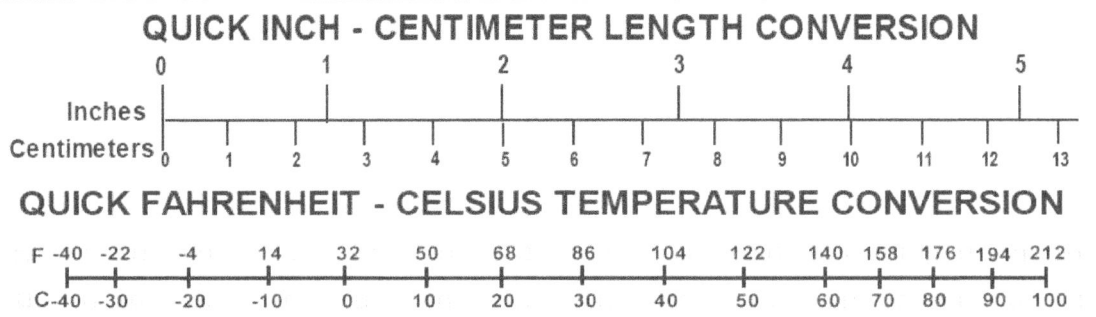

For more exact and or other conversion factors, see NIST Miscellaneous Publication 286, Units of Weights and Measures. Price $2.50 SD Catalog No. C13 10286

Updated 6/17/98

Acknowledgments

The author wishes to express his thanks to Mr. Sean Jacobs and Ms. Julia Greene, student co-ops from the Tufts University Engineering Psychology Program for their assistance in the literature search and data collection for this project. Additional appreciation is extended to Mr. Richard Gopen of Microsys for providing the photographs for this document and to Ms. Anita Graffeo for her editorial assistance. Mr. Dennis Yachechak of FRA's Office of Safety is acknowledged for providing a critical review of this document from the regulator's point of view.

Contents

Illustrations

v

Tables

Executive Summary

Blue flag protection within the railroad industry provides safety to workers by insuring that the equipment they are working on or near is not moved. The procedures have been in place for many years and include the use of a blue flag as a visual indicator that a piece of equipment is not to be moved. Similar precautionary measures have been established in other railroad systems around the world, however, the use of the color blue to designate this safety condition is unique to North America.

Existing Federal regulations for blue safety flags within the railroad industry allow for a wide range of devices to serve as blue flags. The potential this creates for misinterpretation of the safety signal device because of a variety of shades of blue, as well as different shapes, sizes, and placements, increases the risk of an accident to railroad workers. In contrast, safety codes have been designed for and adopted by various industries as a means of standardizing the appearance of safety signals and reducing the risk of injury.

Safety codes include specifications for color, shape, size, text, message content, placement, and other aspects of safety signal devices. The parameters recommended in safety codes are designed to maximize the chances that the target audience will recognize the safety device and take appropriate action. This includes the specification of colors so that the target audience will recognize each color in the code.

An evaluation of commercially available blue signal devices used in the railroad industry was conducted to determine how well current blue flags meet current industry standards. Background color, text size, shape, material, message content, and mounting method were measured and the results analyzed against parameters from safety codes. The results indicated that the majority of devices evaluated did not meet current industrial safety code standards. However, all of the devices met current Federal Railroad Administration (FRA) regulations. The discrepancy between the Federal regulations for blue safety flags and the industrial safety code standards indicates that the railroad industry could benefit from adopting higher standards.

Recommendations for increased standards for railroad blue safety signals are provided that match, to some degree, the standards in existence for other industries and transportation modes, such as highway road signs. Additional recommended specifications include suggested color, letter height, flag shape, message content, materials, and mounting methods.

By using these recommendations as guidelines when designing and purchasing new blue flag devices, on a voluntary basis, the railroad industry will achieve a standardization of blue safety flags. In most cases, these recommendations can be followed at little or no additional cost beyond the cost currently paid for safety flag devices. The benefit to workers, however, will be increased redundancy in the safety signal, which will offer greater recognition of blue flag devices. Additionally, this will benefit railroad company customers who must also operate in the vicinity of rolling stock.

1.   Introduction

Current Federal regulations for blue safety flags within the railroad industry provide for a minimum level of protection to workers from the dangers of moving railroad equipment while it is under repair. The risk to maintenance workers can be extreme under these conditions and a clear signal that a piece of equipment should not be moved is essential to worker safety. To "blue flag" a train has come to mean that a piece of equipment has been appropriately tagged for safety reasons so that it is not moved (Loumiet & Jungbauer, 2005).

Blue flag standards have been developed over many years (U.S. Office of Technology Assessment, 1978) and an elaborate system of rules and regulations exist for the conditions under which blue flags must be displayed (FRA, 2009a). Similar types of rules exist in other railroad systems around the world as well. However, the use of the color blue for this purpose appears to be a North American phenomenon. Many European rail systems rely on the use of "red zones" for worker protection. In Australia, tags are placed at either end of a work zone (Chan & Lau, 2009). Within the Canadian rail system, blue flag protection for workers has been identified recently as a critical component of overall safety management (Coplen & Lee, 2006).

Most references to the blue flag standards emphasize safety concerns for workers and do not specifically address the design characteristics or performance specifications of the flag devices. Although the Federal regulations spell out the procedure for when blue flag protection is required, little guidance exists on what actually may be used as a blue flag. Under the Federal law (FRA, 2009b), blue safety flags must clearly appear to be blue, although no further guidance on specific shades of blue, materials, or shapes is provided. They do not address the type of material. Although some railroad companies may have chosen to enhance the Federal safety regulations by standardizing the shade of blue and providing other uniformities to the specific devices used as blue safety flags, the Federal regulations leave open the possibility of a wide array of devices with various shades of blue to be used for the purpose of maintaining worker safety. Although actual cloth flags appear to have been phased out of use in the railroad industry for the most part, a variety of signs, tags, and lights, as well as other equipment appear to be in current use, such as devices that fold onto the tracks when not in use (referred to in U.S. Patent 7,032,865), blue lights that plug into sockets in the cab (U.S. Patent 4,637,668), and blue strobe lights on the top of locomotives (Columbia & Cowlitz, 2007).

Other high hazard industries often incorporate a high degree of specificity in safety alerting devices, such as tags, warning labels, and signs (e.g., the American National Standards Institute [ANSI] American National Standard for Safety Color Code Z535.1, which was developed by representatives from a variety of industries). Federal regulations and international standards provide specification for safety systems in terms of colors, light levels, shapes, sizes, and materials for safety devices. Some examples include:

- Federal Highway Administration Manual on Traffic Control Devices (Federal Highway Administration, 2006).

- Federal Aviation Administration (2010) – color specifications for aircraft lights.

- ANSI Z535.1 American National Standard for Safety Color Code (American National Standards Institute, 2006).

- ANSI Z535.5 Safety Tags and Barricade Tapes for Temporary Hazards (American National Standards Institute, 2007).

The intent of these regulations is to standardize the appearance and function of warnings. Limiting the possibilities for the design, construction, and implementation of safety devices increases the chances the warning device itself will be identified quickly and correctly by potential users, in turn increasing the likelihood that proper caution will be taken (Chapanis, 1996). This trend to provide higher levels of specification is at odds with the current practice for blue flags in the railroad industry.

The discrepancy between current levels of specificity for blue flags in the Federal railroad regulations and the use of higher levels of specification in other industries raises the question of whether any benefit can be realized in the railroad industry by adopting stricter criteria. This paper provides data from a recently completed review of commercially available blue safety flag devices manufactured for the railroad industry and compares them to existing safety codes supported by various industry groups, government agencies, and international organizations. The results reveal the use of a wide variety of blue safety flag devices, many of which would be considered inappropriate by safety code standards. On the basis of these results, recommendations are made to the railroad industry for the voluntary adoption of a more stringent set of criteria for blue safety flags that is in accordance with international safety codes.

The paper is organized into the following sections:

- Section 1 provides a review of the current Federal regulations.

- Section 2 includes alternative safety color codes and a comparison against the Federal regulations, along with rationale for why other color codes have stricter criteria than the current Federal regulations.

- Section 3 contains additional considerations for safety signal devices, such as size, shape, and materials.

- Section 4 presents data from several existing blue safety flag devices and compares them with existing safety codes.

- Section 5 contains recommendations for a more stringent code to be used in the manufacture and purchase of blue safety flags for the railroad industry.

- Appendix A provides information for designers and purchasing agents within the railroad industry and blue safety flag manufacturers and vendors for use in the procurement and/or development of new blue safety signal devices that will meet the requirements of the voluntary standard that is proposed.

- References.

2.   Current Practice

Current Federal regulations require the use of blue safety signals to protect railroad employees from injury while working on rolling equipment (locomotives and railroad cars). FRA (2009b) spells out several conditions where blue safety signals (or flags) must be displayed as an indication that a maintenance worker is currently working on a piece of equipment. In general, blue safety signals must be displayed on or near the controls of railroad equipment to provide a signal to any potential operator that the equipment is not to be moved. Blue flag protection also applies to remote control operations, such as the activities in rail yards. The use of remote control operations in which the operator is remotely located from the actual equipment being moved increases the need for the coordination of blue flag protection procedures to ensure safety. Further consideration of the topic of blue flag protection in remote control operations, however, is beyond the scope of this document.

As mentioned, little guidance exists as to actually what constitutes a blue safety flag. The relevant content states that:

> "Blue signal means a clearly distinguishable blue flag or blue light by day and a blue light at night. When attached to the operating controls of a locomotive, it need not be lighted if the inside of the cab area of the locomotive is sufficiently lighted so as to make the blue signal clearly distinguishable."

The Federal regulations leave open the possibility of a wide range of objects in any shade of blue serving as a blue safety flag.

According to Dreyfus (1972), the use of blue as a safety color in the railroad industry has a long history dating back to the 1800s. Over time, the use of the color blue has come to symbolize safety, among other meanings, when applied to signs and signals as indicated in Figure 1. Within the United States, for example, blue signs are used to identify hospitals, and blue lights are used on police vehicles. This meaning of blue has been adopted internationally as well, with other nations incorporating the use of blue into safety codes. For example, the Australian color code for physical hazards specifies the use of blue on signs for mandatory safety instructions, and for designating physical areas in which specific safety procedures must be followed (Standards Association of Australia, 1985).

Figure 1. Images of Different Uses of Blue in Commonly Observed Signs and Signals

4

The use of blue as a safety color becomes more complicated, however, when considering the many shades of blue that exist. Navy blue, robin's egg blue, and turquoise all retain an essential appearance of blueness despite their unique appearances. All three of these shades would potentially qualify under the current Federal regulations as long as the person viewing the safety flag interpreted the color as a shade of blue. Complicating the problem are individual differences between observers, particularly those due to losses of visual sensitivity with advancing age (e.g., progressive loss of sensitivity to short wave stimulation due to the yellowing the lens in the human eye) and disease (e.g., diabetic retinopathy) that limit color appearance. What may appear sufficiently blue to one observer may not to another, and what may appear blue to a younger worker may not appear blue to the same worker later in her or his career.

The Federal regulations also allow for a wide interpretation of the actual materials that can be used as a safety flag. Informal surveys with railroad employees have revealed that in some cases the current Federal regulations have allowed some unconventional devices to be used, such as a blue awning from a building being wrapped around the controls of a locomotive. Whereas this application may have been effective, the potential effectiveness of other unconventional devices is less apparent. One locomotive engineer reported that his railroad paints the washers blue and places them around control levers. Variations in the paint used, the size of washers, and the visibility of the washers potentially reduce the effectiveness of this specific safety flag. Although this application may meet the letter of the regulation, it leaves open a range of interpretations to anyone who is unfamiliar with that specific application, as well as the possibility that the washer will not be seen at all.

The Federal regulations also call for all locomotive engineers to pass a color vision test as part of the requirements for working in the field. A list of acceptable color vision tests for locomotive engineers is provided by FRA (2009c). Several of these tests, however, do not test for the perception of the color blue. Although color vision deficiencies of this type are relatively rare, it is presently possible for an engineer to qualify for work without having to prove that he or she can distinguish blue among other colors, depending on the color vision test used. Also, a railroad worker may possibly lose the ability to discriminate some colors through an acquired color deficiency. For example, this can happen as a complication of diabetes. When the ability to discriminate colors is lost, additional information is needed to ensure that an employee can identify the object as a blue safety flag.

The rationale behind the current blue flag standards have developed over time. The regulations have not been updated to reflect newer technologies, developments in safety standards, and testing methods. A safety review from 1978 indicated that the existing blue flag regulations were not developed on the basis of any proven methodology that would lead to improvements in safety (U.S. Office of Technology Assessment, 1978). Since that time, the Canadian rail system has attempted to modify its blue flag standards (U.S. Office of Technology Assessment, 1979). Canadian blue flags now must meet the following criteria (Transport Canada, 2001):

- Mounted on a pole
- Affixed to the rail
- Five feet above the top of the rail
- Positioned at right angles to the rail
- Royal blue
- 18-inch square

These requirements do not cover all potential conditions, such as tags at the controls in the cab; however, they do specify several parameters for blue flags that are currently lacking in U.S. standards.

In addition to the specification of the blue flags, the Canadian National Railway Company (CN) also requires that only specific CN personnel place and remove blue flags from railroad equipment. This practice ensures that the person placing equipment in "blue flag status" is the same person who takes it out of that status, adding a measure of safety. This policy is particularly important when CN personnel are interacting with customers who may not be familiar with the current safety concerns in the vicinity of the rail equipment (Canadian National Railway Company, 2006). It should be noted that FRA regulations are consistent with this requirement.

3. Safety Color Codes

Safety color codes have been developed and adopted in several industries and safety applications. The general intent of a safety color code is to provide an unambiguous signal to an operator of a system—through the use of color—regarding safety concerns. Color codes usually use a limited set of colors, ranging from 4 to 7 depending on the application (International Commission on Illumination, 1975; Smallman & Boynton, 1993; Cardosi, 1998). The primary objective of limiting the size of the color set is to minimize the amount of information the user has to remember. Additionally, the colors chosen are common color names such as red, green, yellow, and blue, rather than names like rose, evergreen, amber, and aqua. The specific colors chosen for use in a signal must have the appearance of the color name being represented. That is, when a viewer sees a signal of a particular color, the appearance of the colored signal must bring to mind the correct color name. Red signals must look red to the viewer. Similarly, green signals must look green, yellow signals must look yellow, and blue signals must look blue. Although this aspect of safety color codes may seem obvious, it also requires that some limits be set to define what the acceptable shades of each color are that will qualify to be used within the code.

To specify shades of color for a color code, a color measurement system is needed to allow for accurate color naming and reproduction. The left panel of Figure 2 depicts the chromaticity diagram defined by the International Commission on Illumination (CIE), which provides a quantitative and spatial method for describing color. According to the CIE, all visible colors can be specified by a pair of x, y coordinates. The x and y numbers are dimensionless values that are mathematically derived from equations that emulate the amount of excitation of the three different photosensitive receptors in the eye. When plotted as coordinates in a graph, any color can be plotted in this diagram according to its x and y values. Monochromatic or single wavelength light (i.e., the most pure colors possible) plots are along the outer curve of the diagram. Less saturated colors plot toward the interior of the diagram with white plotting near the center.

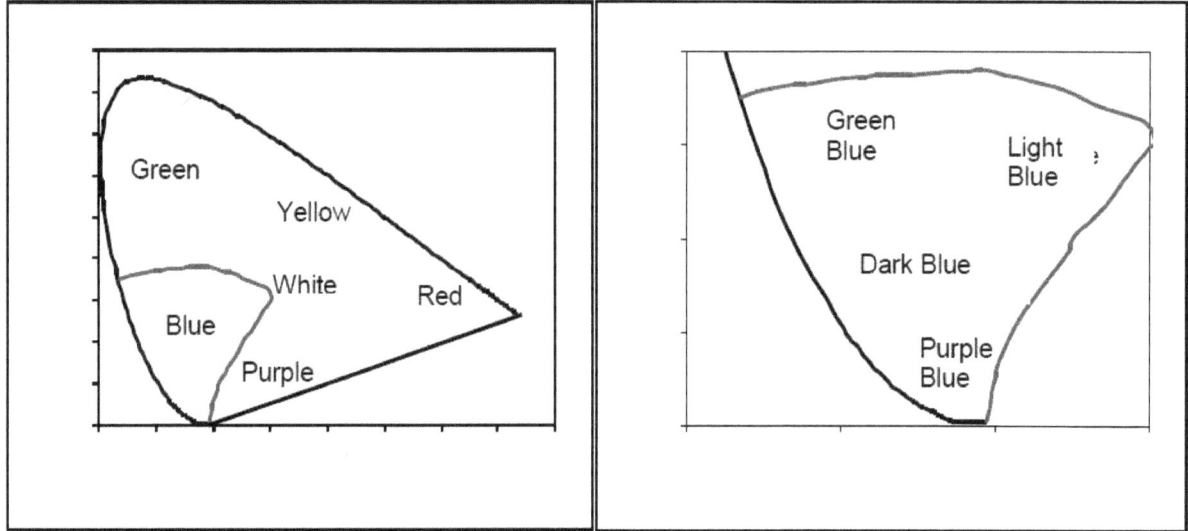

Figure 2. Relationship between the Munsell Color System and the CIE System. The left panel of the CIE 1930 Chromaticity Diagram shows that the x, y coordinates plot visible colors and that monochromatic light plots along the black curve. Color labels indicate regions where different colors are plotted. The blue outline encloses the plot area for all shades of blue in the Munsell system. The right panel displays an enlargement of the enclosed area for the Munsell system. Shades of blue are labeled within the enclosed area. (Munsell data downloaded from: http://www.cis.rit.edu/mcsl/online/munsell_data/all.dat)

An advantage of the CIE color measurement system is that it allows for colors to be measured using calibrated instruments and for quantitative data on colors to be exchanged between manufacturers. However, the CIE system does not readily allow for an appreciation of color appearance, and alternative color specification systems have been developed to fill this need. The Munsell color measurement system, for example, provides a descriptive color naming system that specifies colors with three parameters (Chapanis, 1996). Hue is specified with color names (e.g., red, blue, purple, etc.), while the value (i.e., the dimension from light to dark) is represented on a scale from 1 to 10, and chroma (i.e., the dimension from pale to vivid) is also represented on a numeric scale.

The enclosed area within the CIE diagram in the left panel of Figure 2 shows the relationship between the Munsell color system and the CIE system. The enclosed area is magnified in the right panel. All of the colors within the Munsell system with some blue appearance have x, y coordinates that lie within the enclosed area. The labels within the diagram show the range of color appearances that are possible from green-blue to purple blue and from lighter blue to darker blue. Many of the colors falling in this region meet the requirement within the Federal regulations of having a blue appearance, although they may not all be suitable shades of blue for a blue signal, because they may also have the appearance of another color, such as purple or green (e.g., blue-green).

Through the use of a color measurement system, shades of colors can be specified that have distinct appearances that correspond with color names. Therefore, specific shades of blue can be chosen and specified as a subregion within all of the shades of blue. When used within a color safety code, this subregion defines all of the shades of blue that would be acceptable blue signals. That is, these are all of the shades of blue that look blue to observers, and not slightly green or purple, or dark or light, et cetera.

Many existing safety color codes use the CIE chromaticity system as a means of insuring that signal devices have an unambiguous color appearance. These codes have been developed for use in a variety of industries and safety applications. Several are described here along with descriptions of additional documents produced by standards organizations for use in the specification of colors.

SAE AS25050 Colors, Aeronautical Lights and Lighting Equipment, General Requirements For – A safety color code adopted by the Society of Automotive Engineers (SAE) for use in aviation applications, including signal lights. The color code includes three specifications for blue signals: aviation blue, blue filters over white lights, and identification blue. The use of identification blue is intended to ensure that the signal is perceived as blue and no other color (Society of Automotive Engineers, 1998).

SAA Industrial Safety Colour Code (AS 1318-1985) – Standards Association of Australia (SAA) provides a standard for the Use of Colour for the Marking of Physical Hazards and the Identification of Certain Equipment in Industry (Standards Association of Australia, 1985).

ANSI Z535.1 – A color code developed for a variety of industrial applications. This standard has been adopted by the Pipeline and Hazardous Materials Safety Administration for use in hazardous materials labeling. ANSI Z535.1 also includes the specification of "safety blue," a unique, reproducible blue that is highly recognizable (American National Standards Institute, 2006).

CIE 39.2 Recommendations for Surface Colours for Visual Signaling – A set of recommended colors to be used for a variety of color signaling applications (International Commission on Illumination, 1983).

CIE 107-1994 – Review of the Official Recommendations of the CIE for the Colours of Signal Lights – Incorporates additional recommendations to existing color codes with special considerations for blue signals among others. Precautions are provided for insuring that light blue signals are not confused with white (International Commission on Illumination, 1994).

CIE 74-1988 Roadsigns – Provides a discussion of many factors that influence roadsign perception, including color (International Commission on Illumination, 1988).

CIE 2.2 – 1995 Colors of Light Signals – Provides recommendations for the use of colors in signal systems, and includes a discussion of the difficulties of perceiving blue signals (International Commission on Illumination, 1995).

Federal Highway Administration (2006) – Traffic control devices on Federal aid and other streets and highways; color specifications for retroreflective sign and pavement marking materials. Provides color specifications for these traffic control devices.

The CIE x, y coordinates for the recommended shades of blue from these standards and supporting documents are plotted in Figure 3. In most cases, rather than recommending specific x, y values, a range of values is given. These areas are labeled within the diagram. The curves represent the chromaticity areas that specify blue within different safety color codes: ANSI Z535.1 – Solid Blue, SAE AS25050 – Solid Purple, SAA – Dashed Purple, CIE 2.2 1985 – Dashed Blue, CIE 107 1994 – Dashed Dark Blue, CIE 74 1988 – Dashed Gray.

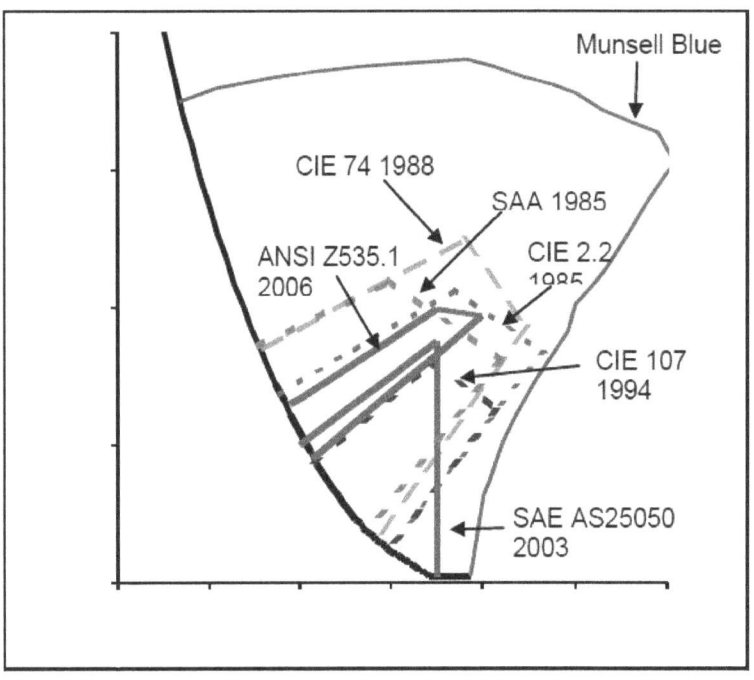

Figure 3. Enlargement of the Portion of the CIE Chromaticity Diagram for Shades of Blue as Defined by the Munsell Color System

The area for the entire range of blue colors, as defined by the Munsell system, is also replotted in Figure 3 for comparison to the recommendations from the various color standards. It can be seen in this diagram that the gamut of colors that are used within established safety color codes is much smaller than the entire gamut of colors that have a blue appearance. The reason for the reduced gamut for the blue signals within safety color codes is that these specified shades of blue have been determined to be highly recognizable shades of blue and are not likely to be confused with other colors (American National Standards Institute, 2006).

Comparison of the plots in Figure 2 and Figure 3 reveal that the gamut of blue safety colors have been chosen, in part, to minimize the potential for a blue signal to appear white or green to an observer. The left panel of Figure 2 shows that blue, green and white regions of the color space border each other. The right panel indicates that a gradual appearance change occurs from white to light blue to dark blue moving horizontally across the diagram and from green to blue green to dark blue moving vertically through the diagram. Figure 3 shows that the concentration of blue safety chromaticities is located away from the light blue and blue green regions, reducing the chance that a blue signal may be confused with white or green.

Further inspection of the specific plots for the different safety color codes shows that different standards have used different criteria for defining the boundaries of acceptable blue signals. The most stringent criteria have been adopted by ANSI Z535.1, as can be seen by the small area defining safety blue for this standard. Adopting this color code, as an example, would ensure that all blue flags would meet most—and sometimes all—of the existing color codes. Meeting criteria for all of the color codes is harder. Close inspection of Figure 3 shows that all of the color code gamuts illustrated have some overlap, or, as in the case of ANSI Z535.1 and CIE 107 1994, share a border. This narrow region in the CIE diagram contains shades of blue that are acceptable under all color codes, indicating the potential for the selection of an ideal shade of blue that would be acceptable under all color codes. This may not be a practical application, however, requiring a carefully controlled manufacturing process that would unnecessarily increase cost.

Visual Performance Properties of Blue Safety Flags

In addition to the specification of colors, safety signals also often have additional requirements to ensure that they will be visible under all conditions. The American National Standards Institute (2007) provides standards for temporary hazard tags that may be applicable to blue safety flags. Temporary hazards include equipment lockout procedures that prevent operation of machinery, similar to the blue flag protection in the railroad industry. Several properties of safety tag devices are considered below:

- The size of safety tags should be determined, in part by the size of the letters used for hazard labels. Text sizes are based, in part on viewing distance and on viewing conditions. The required letter height for reading increases directly with viewing distance, as do the overall dimensions of the tag. For viewing distances less than 4 feet (ft), a minimum letter size of 0.16 inches (in) is suggested for favorable reading conditions, and a size of 0.34 in is suggested for unfavorable viewing conditions. At a distance of 10 ft, the letter sizes increase to 0.4 and 0.84 in, respectively. The overall size must also be sufficient to allow all of the text to be clearly displayed without crowding of the letters.

- Rectangles are the recommended shape of safety tags. The corners can be square or rounded. The rectangular tag provides a background for printed safety symbols such as triangles that convey additional information to the viewer.

- Safety tags should be attached directly to the controls in the operator's direct view to prevent the operator from using machinery during lockout procedures.

- Safety tags should be made of durable material, such as plastic or metal. The tags should be attached with nylon fasteners.

- Safety tags contain standardized text and symbols that convey information about the hazard. A warning symbol and hazard label, such as "danger" indicate the potential for death or bodily injury if the hazard is not avoided. Additional information can tell the operator direct actions to perform or to avoid.

Temporary hazard safety tags have standardized shapes, colors, and messages. Standardization removes any ambiguity about the intention of the tag. The American National Standards

Institute (2007) suggests the use of red for extreme hazards in which death could result and reserves blue for hazard notices. However, the long-standing use of blue within the railroad industry suggests that, at least within this industry, the meaning of the color blue is known and that standardizing the size, shape, location, and possibly the materials that can be used for blue safety flags, as well as the shade of blue, will generate uniformity throughout the railroad industry. This will reduce the chance that a well intended, but potentially ineffective object—like a blue painted washer—will be used as a blue safety signal.

4. Analysis of Existing Blue Safety Flags

Several commercially available blue safety flag devices were analyzed with respect to existing safety color codes and safety device visual performance properties. The results of this analysis reveal a wide range of devices that qualify as blue safety flags and point toward the potential benefit to the railroad industry from adopting a stricter set of criteria for defining blue safety flags.

Signal devices were purchased from several vendors advertising blue safety signals for use in the railroad industry. Because the intention of this analysis was to identify a range of blue safety flags available to the railroad industry, the choice of safety flags was based on recommendations from railroad companies, observations of the actual devices seen in operation at different train yards, and the recommendations of manufacturers and suppliers. The choice of blue flags tested is not intended to represent the most common practice within the railroad industry, but rather, a range of potential devices that meet the Federal regulations and that are currently commercially available. As mentioned earlier, many railroad companies augment the Federal requirements with additional specifications for blue safety flags.

The specific devices that were analyzed are listed in Table 1 along with the chromaticity coordinates, the physical dimensions, shape, methods for mounting in the environment, and the materials from which they were made. Chromaticity measurements were made in both direct and indirect sunlight with a PhotoResearch PR650 Spectroradiometer, which had been recently calibrated.

The chromaticity coordinates of the blue flag devices are plotted in Figure 4 along with the blue color boundaries for the blue gamut of the Munsell system and three of the existing safety color codes. Chromaticity coordinates for a product that fall within the area of a safety code in Figure 4 indicate that the product meets the color specification for that code.

All 11 products have chromaticities within the blue gamut of the Munsell system. However, only 6 out of 11 plot within the area of the CIE 74 88 & 39.2 83 color code, one of the least restrictive of the safety color codes. Three of the products, the dark blue light, the blue tape, and the "safety first" sign plot within the gamut for the ANSI Z535.1 code, with only the latter two plotting within the range for the SAE AS25050 code. These results indicate that approximately half of the existing blue flag products evaluated had highly recognizable shades of blue with only two or three meeting the strictest criteria. Five of the analyzed blue flag devices plot well away from the safety code areas. As the color of these products gets closer to the right edge of the Munsell blue gamut area, the blue appearance becomes potentially confused with white under some lighting conditions.

13

Table 1. Properties of Blue Flag Products

		Product Type	Message*	Chromaticity Coordinates		Shape	Width (inches)	Height (inches)	Mount	Material
				x	y					
7		Dark blue flag		.293	.294**	Rectangular	18	18	Wooden dowel	Cloth
5		Light blue flag		.231	.274	Rectangular	13	11.5	Wooden dowel	Cloth
6		Medium blue flag	"Safety First"	.195	.158	Rectangular	18	18	Metal pole with magnetic base	Rubber/ vinyl
3		Dark blue flashing light		.181	.188	Cylindrical	3.75 (diameter)	5.5	Magnetic base	Plastic lens
4		Light blue flashing light		.166	.209	Round	7 (diameter)		Magnetic base	Plastic lens
1		Sign	"Danger Men Working on This Track"	.228	.289	Rectangular	15	12	Pole mount to rail	Metal
9		Sign	"Danger Men Working on This Track"	.190	.238	Rectangular	15	12		Metal
10		Sign	"Safety First"	.153	.143	Rectangular	15	12		Metal
2		Sign	"STOP"	.262	.307	Rectangular				Metal
11			"Stop Men at Work"	.200	.276	Rectangular	14	12	Pole mount to rail	Metal
8		Blue tape		.167	.169	Rectangular	1.5			Vinyl

* All messages were displayed in white text on a blue background.
** This product was purchased as a dark blue flag. The chromaticity coordinates, however, indicate more of a neutral color. What has most likely happened is that as the reflectance was reduced to achieve the dark appearance the range of chromaticities was also reduced.

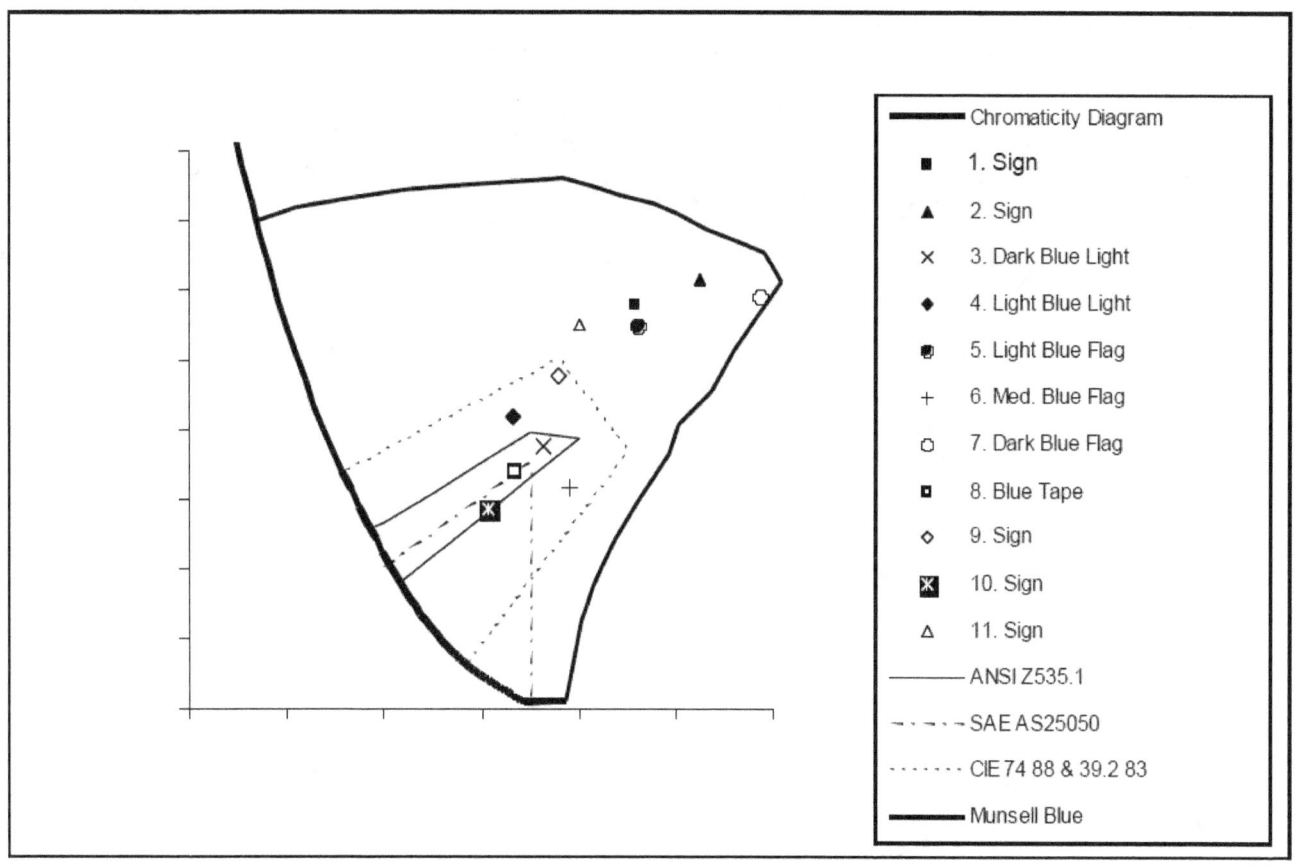

Figure 4. Plot of Chromaticity Coordinates of Blue Flag Products

The solid thick line shows the left edge of the chromaticity diagram. The medium solid line shows the gamut of blue colors in the Munsell system. The small dashed line is the safety code for CIE 74 88 & 39.2 83. The solid thin line is the safety code for ANSI Z535.1. The alternating dash – dot line is the safety code for SAE AS25050. Chromaticity coordinates for specific blue flag products that plot within the bounds of a safety code meet the blue specification for that code.

Table 2 provides a complete comparison of all 11 of the blue safety flags evaluated against all of the safety color codes illustrated in Figure 3. A review of the information indicates that many devices meet the criteria for some of the codes but not all. Only one of the devices, sign 10, meets the criteria for all of the color codes listed. Its chromaticity coordinates lie on the border between ANSI 535.1 and CIE 107 1994, as well as within the range for all of the other color codes. Five of the 11 products meet none of the safety codes.

15

Table 2. Comparison of Blue Safety Products by Safety Code

Product Type		CIE 74 1988	CIE 2.2 1985	SAA 1985	ANSI Z535.1 2006	SAE AS25050	CIE 107 1994
10	SAFETY FIRST	●	●	●	●	●	●
8		●	●	●	●	●	
3		●	●	●	●		
6	SAFETY FIRST	●	●	●			
4		●					
9	DANGER MEN WORKING ON THIS TRACK	●					
1	DANGER MEN WORKING ON THIS TRACK						
2	STOP						
5							
7							
11	STOP MEN AT WORK						

Section 2 and Figure 4 illustrate how the selection of a color code limits the possible choices of shades of blue for use in safety devices. Five of the commercially available products evaluated did not meet the criteria for any color codes. These products would not be considered acceptable if a safety color code were adopted by the railroad industry. The six products that did meet the criteria for at least one safety code would be acceptable depending on which code was adopted. As criteria become more stringent, fewer of the existing devices are acceptable. For example, six devices meet the color criteria under CIE 74 1988, but only three are acceptable according to ANSI Z535.1. In the strictest case, when the overlapping areas for all six color codes are used, only one device is acceptable. However, meeting the criteria for multiple color codes is not a criterion for safety. Rather, the limitation of the range of colors that a specific code requires is what improves safety by only allowing a small amount of variation in the shade of the specified color. When the variation in color appearance is limited, the recognition of the color is increased.

A comparison of the physical dimensions and shape properties of the set of analyzed blue safety flags reveal them to be of similar size (approximately 180-square in), and shape (i.e., rectangular), although one of the lights was round. The materials from which they were made differ widely, although none had highly glossy surfaces that would make them difficult to recognize in sunlight. None of the tested devices utilized retroreflective materials. Retroreflectivity is not a blue flag requirement because it is primarily a property that affects night time signal detection when a light is shone on the material. The FRA regulations call for the use of lights or lighted cabs at night. The different flags mounted in various ways, including some with poles and mounting brackets for attaching to the rails, others with magnetic bases for mounting on the side of a locomotive cab, and still others with wooden dowels suggesting the need for an additional flag stand for the device to be properly mounted.

Six of the products included text, providing additional warning information to the viewer. Table 3 provides a breakdown of the text properties on these blue flag devices. The device numbers are provided in the first column, adjacent to the message. Three letter heights are provided, large, medium, and small, to accommodate the different text sizes in the most complex message. Both letter height and stroke width, in inches, are provided. The estimated viewing distance for favorable and unfavorable viewing conditions are listed for each letter height category. The last column indicates whether or not the message content meets the criteria listed in ANSI Z535.5 for Safety Tags and Barricade Tapes.

The information in Table 3 reveals a variety of text sizes in use on blue safety flags. The estimated viewing distances were calculated for favorable and unfavorable viewing conditions based on formulas provided in ANSI Z535.5. Favorable viewing conditions provide a clear, unobstructed view of the flag in well-lighted conditions in an uncluttered environment. Viewing distance is equal to 25 times the letter height under these conditions. Unfavorable viewing conditions require larger letters at the same viewing distance, determined by multiplying the letter height by 0.084.

According to ANSI Z535.5, the letter height on a safety device determines the viewing distance required for safety. On the basis of the need to be able to read all of the text, the letter heights on the devices in Table 3 collectively indicate a safe viewing distance of approximately 20 ft is implied. The ANSI standard also provides recommendations for the message content on safety devices. In addition to a signal word, information instructing the user what to do or what not to do should be included as well. None of the devices evaluated met these criteria.

Notably, the blue flag requirements in FRA, 49 CFR 218 (2009), do not explicitly require text. The term blue flag appears to be a holdover from a time when blue cloth flags were used. Blue metal signs appear to have replaced cloth flags in more recent practice. Blue lights are called for at night. Therefore, blue flags are primarily identified by their "blueness" and not by any particular wording that may be placed on them. However, FRA does recognize the value of text and recommends the use of "out of service" tags for use on cab control stands in some applications (ENSCO, 2007). No criteria are provided for these tags, and when compared to ANSI Z535.5, this type of tag message would not meet the criteria either.

Table 3. Text Properties of Blue Flag Products

| | Message | Large | | Medium | | Small | | Meets ANSI Z535.5 Message Content Criteria |
		Letter Height/ Stroke Width*	Estimated Viewing Distance** Favorable/ Unfavorable	Letter Height/ Stroke Width*	Estimated Viewing Distance** Favorable/ Unfavorable	Letter Height/ Stroke Width*	Estimated Viewing Distance** Favorable/ Unfavorable	
1	"Danger Men Working on This Track"	4.1/0.6	103/49	2.0/0.3	50/24	1.6/0.3	40/19	No
2	"STOP"							No
6	"Safety First"	3.0/0.4	75/36					No
9	"Danger Men Working on This Track"	2.8/0.7	70/33			1.4/0.4	35/17	No
10	"Safety First"	3.6/0.6	90/43					No
11	"Stop Men at Work"	4.0/0.6	100/48			1.9/0.3	48/23	No

* Units are in inches.
** Units are in feet.

Table 4 summarizes the results of several parameters of the evaluated safety flags and compares them against FRA and safety code criteria, including color, shape, material, mounting, and text.

The contents of Table 4 show that all 11 devices meet FRA's criteria because the shade of blue is not an FRA requirement. Specification according to one of the safety codes would result in five of the devices evaluated here being rejected for not appearing to be blue. When compared to safety color codes, and the safety tag criteria in ANSI Z535.5, only the two lights, devices 3 and 4, meet all of the criteria. Because lights do not have to meet criteria for shape, material, and text, these other criteria do not apply. In a stricter interpretation, using ANSI Z535.1 as the color code, only device 3 would actually qualify.

Table 4. Blue Flag Product Ratings by FRA Criteria and Industry Safety Codes

Device		Description	Number of Safety Color Codes met	Meets FRA Criteria (Blue Flag or Light)	Shape (Rectangular)	Material (metal or plastic)	Mounting Device	Meets Safety Code Recommended Text Specifications
7		Flag	0	Yes	Yes	No	No	No
5		Flag	0	Yes	Yes	No	No	No
6		Flag	3	Yes	Yes	Yes	Yes	No
3		Light	4	Yes	N/A	N/A*	Yes	N/A
4		Light	1	Yes	N/A	N/A*	Yes	N/A
1		Sign	0	Yes	Yes	Yes	Yes	No
9		Sign	1	Yes	Yes	Yes	Yes	No
10		Sign	6	Yes	Yes	Yes	Yes	No
2		Sign	0	Yes	Yes	Yes	Yes	No
11		Sign	0	Yes	Yes	Yes	Yes	No
8		Tape	5	Yes	N/A	Yes	No	No

* N/A – These products are lights. Safety codes do not specifically address the materials required for lighted devices beyond color specifications for any filters or light sources.

Comparing the criteria for acceptance as a blue safety flag device between FRA regulations and safety codes and standards reveals that many more devices qualify under FRA rules than would qualify under the criteria offered by industry standards. The main criterion for FRA is blueness, and even this is not well specified. If FRA were to adopt a stricter interpretation of the definition of blue that is consistent with an established safety code, then about half, if not more of the devices evaluated, would not qualify. Extending the criteria to include text for nonlighted devices eliminates all but the two lights that were evaluated. On the basis of established safety standards, blueness as a property is insufficient by itself for the specification of signs, tags, and perhaps, other safety tag devices.

5.   Recommended Standards for Blue Safety Signal Devices

The existence of standards for the specification of safety devices—such as warning labels, signs, tags, lights, and tapes—indicates that value can be gained from uniformity when conveying warning messages. A similar appearance in terms of color, shape, size, and message reduces the chance that a message will be misinterpreted and leads to actions that could jeopardize employees working under the protection of blue signals. This makes learning the meaning of the warning easier and reduces the training requirements. By exacting a standard that reserves a particular color, shape, size, and other product specifications that avoid similarity with other objects used in the railroad environment, we reduce the likelihood that employees will make an error and fail to recognize the warning. The alternative is the possibility of idiosyncratic features that can result from the decisions made by individual designers. The variety of colors in the blue flags that were evaluated shows how easily this happens.

Uniformity of blue safety flags will benefit railroad workers by reducing the variability that may exist. Standard colors, shapes, and messages provide redundancy to the signal conveyed by the blue safety flag. When considering human performance, an increase in redundancy reduces the overall information content of the signal, which in turn reduces the time required for the message to be interpreted (Wickens & Hollands, 2000).

Redundancy also offers additional protection in case an aspect of the flag is missed. For example, a railroad worker with an acquired color vision deficiency will benefit from a standard message and shape to the blue flag in the event that he or she is unable to distinguish blue from other colors. The inclusion of redundancy will also be of benefit to the customers of railroads, such as truck drivers and other people in the transportation industry who have to interact with different railroads in different locations. These people are not as familiar with railroad operations and will more easily interpret blue flag restrictions if the same blue flag devices are seen everywhere they operate on railroad territory.

The following recommendations are offered for consideration as a standard for future blue flag devices. As existing products are replaced, the use of these recommendations in the design and acquisition of new devices will eventually lead to more uniform use of blue flag safety throughout the railroad industry. Importantly, these recommendations refer only to the blue safety flag devices themselves and are not a substitution for any other safety devices that may be used in the railroad industry as part of the overall blue flag protection process, such as interlocks for the prevention of inadvertent operation of a locomotive or the use of throttle disabling devices:

1. Color Specification – *Specify the acceptable color or range of colors using a color specification system or select an existing safety color code standard for the specification of the color of blue safety flags.*

    There are three approaches to picking a color specification. An existing color code can be used (e.g., ANSI Z535.1). Alternatively, a specific color can be chosen. Two options for this approach include the use of safety blue, or the use of the Canadian standard of royal blue. Each of these approaches is discussed.

    a. Using a color code requires that the manufacturer of the blue flag produce a shade of blue with chromaticity coordinates that fall within the range allowed. The purchaser must either rely on the manufacturer to ensure that this happens or be able to independently verify that the color meets the specifications. Manufacturers can meet the criteria by using established products with specific color properties, such as reflective sheeting with known chromaticity coordinates. Most manufacturers of reflective materials specify the color properties of their products in accordance with ASTM regulations. Conventional printing ink can be used as well; however, the manufacturer will have to find a way to independently verify the chromaticity of the product. This approach is likely to be the most costly of the three considered here.

b. A second approach is to use safety blue, which is a predetermined color that has already been verifiably matched using conventional printing methods (ANSI Z535). Safety blue is already in high use because it has been incorporated into sign standards by the Federal Highway Administration. The Manual of Uniform Traffic Control Devices (Federal Highway Administration, 2006) specifies the use of safety blue for specific highway and roadway signs, making safety blue a well-defined and highly recognizable shade of blue by most if not all railroad workers. This is likely to be a low-cost solution, no more than the cost of producing existing blue flag devices.

c. A third approach is to utilize the royal blue specification adopted by the Canadian railway system. Although the Canadian specifications for blue flags do not provide additional criteria for the reproduction of royal blue, the concept is similar to the use of safety blue provided that standard printing inks can be used. This alternative has the advantage of providing uniformity between the United States and Canada. Depending on the difficulty of specifying royal blue, this approach is likely to have a low to intermediate cost.

2. Blue Flag Size – *Specify minimum blue flag sizes to be used in different locations based on the required distance to be seen by the potential viewer at each location.*

According to ANSI Z535.5, the size of the device is dictated by the size of the text that is printed on it. The safe viewing distance determines text size. The analysis above indicated that the existing products had letter sizes that accommodate a safe viewing distance of 20 ft. FRA regulations as well as the American National Standards Institute standard indicate that blue flags should be placed on controls to reduce the chance of inadvertent operation. Therefore, a range of blue flag sizes is required. The guiding principle for size, therefore, is to provide information to viewers at a sufficient size so that it can be read at a safe distance to minimize the chance that the rail equipment in blue flag status will be moved. Within the locomotive cab this may include smaller tags that are placed on the control stand which can be read from a distance that will minimize the chance that a potential operator will get close enough to start operating the equipment before realizing that blue flag protection was established. Under ideal viewing conditions, a viewing distance of 4 ft requires a minimum of 12-point type. When viewing conditions are unfavorable because reduced visibility (e.g., poor lighting and weather), the point size increases to 24.

<u>Message Content</u> – *Specify a standard message format and content for blue safety flags.*

ANSI Z535.5 indicates four essential components to a warning message. First, a signal word is needed that indicates the level of hazard. It is printed in capital letters. The word "danger" is suggested for situations in which a high probability exists that death or serious injury will occur. Second, a safety symbol is included to provide pictorial emphasis. An exclamation embedded in an upright triangle is recommended. Other symbol options are available in ANSI Z535.3-2007. The third component is a word message. It conveys three specific elements, including a statement of the hazard (e.g., men working), an action statement to avoid the hazard (e.g., do not operate), and a consequence statement of what will happen if the warning is ignored (e.g., lives are on the line). An example is provided in Appendix A. The fourth component is a signature block that indicates who placed the flag, the date it was placed, the expected removal date, and any other pertinent information. Additional specifications on word spacing and formatting are provided within the standard. Examples include:

<u>Text Justification and Spacing</u>

This is an example of a word message with proper leading and word/letter spacing.	This is an example of a word message with too much leading and too much word/letter spacing.	This is an example of a word message with not enough leading and not enough word/letter spacing.
Example 1 - Proper spacing between lines and characters.	Example 2 - Too much space between lines and characters.	Example 3 - Not enough space between lines and characters.

3. <u>Flag Shape</u> – *Standardize the shape of blue safety flags.*

The recommended shape is rectangular with either square or rounded corners. Most of the evaluated blue flag devices already incorporated this requirement. Two of the devices were squares, however, and this is the shape specified in the Canadian regulations. Whereas in geometric terms, squares and rectangles are special cases of quadrilateral shapes, and the distinct difference in appearance is worth noting. Consistency with American National Standards Institute criteria dictates the use of rectangles with one pair of sides longer than the other. Adhering to Canadian standards requires all sides to be of the same length. Because these two shapes are not visually identical—for the sake of consistency—the use of one or the other is recommended.

4. Flag Materials – *Standardize the materials used for blue safety flags in different applications, including exterior and interior use.*

For the most part, cloth flags are no longer used within the industry (Bogart, 2006). The availability of blue flags from suppliers suggests, however, that specification of materials is important to ensure that the correct product is obtained. Metal signs have high durability for use outside. These are typically fastened to a pole that is mounted to a rail. Within cabs, however, other materials will likely be more effective, such as hard plastic that are not as heavy and more easily carried into a cab. One of the evaluated devices was made from a rubberized vinyl. The claim is made that the material is durable for outside use and light enough for inside use. Similar materials are used in temporary highway signs.

5. Flag Mounting – *Standardize the way blue safety flags are mounted to ensure their security as well as their visibility to potential viewers.*

The way blue flags are mounted has a direct impact on whether they will be seen. Several possibilities are to be considered with regard to the way a flag is mounted, including:

a. Signs mounted on posts that are attached to rails hold the sign at a specific height above the top of the rail. The Canadian regulations specify a height of 5 ft. The flags also must be mounted at a right angle to the track so that a person approaching the equipment along the track will face the flag. All of the signs evaluated could be mounted on poles that attach to the rails.

b. Both FRA regulations and ANSI Z535.5 specify that blue safety flags should be placed on or near the controls. In the locomotive cab, therefore, tags must be mounted on or near the control stand to prevent an operator from activating controls inappropriately.

c. ANSI Z535.5 further suggests attaching flags to controls in a way that restricts the movement of the control. The use of plastic tie wraps as fasteners is recommended. These can be fastened in a way that prohibits the activation of the controls.

d. Two of the flags evaluated were attached to wooden dowels, making it unclear how they would be used in operation. The design and procurement of blue flag devices, therefore, must also include the method and materials for mounting them.

e. One of the flags and the two lights that were evaluated had magnetic bases that can be used to attach the flag to a rail or any piece of metal on the rail equipment. Magnets are convenient to some extent because they do not require any tools for application or removal. However, devices attached with magnets can be easily displaced when bumped, suggesting that they should not be used in place of a sturdier mounting device.

6. Blue Lights – *Standardize the shade of blue for blue safety lights.*

   Although both of the lights evaluated had colors that mapped within safety color code ranges, blue lights can possibly appear white under some circumstances depending on the technology that is used. Conventional lights use a white light source covered by a plastic blue filter. In theory, the filter blocks light in the red portion of the spectrum and allows the energy in the blue portion to pass to the observer, therefore, generating a blue appearance. The relative energy of the light source in the different portions of the spectrum and the effectiveness of the filter, however, combine in reality to determine color appearance. In many cases, these nominally blue lights have a white spot in the center and appear bluer toward the edges. To overcome this problem, the supplier must provide a light that is uniform in appearance and that has a blue appearance that falls within the range of a safety code. The use of blue light-emitting diodes overcomes this problem in many cases.

7. Restrictions on the Use of Blue – *Limit the use of blue in all color codes used on railroad territory so that it only can be used for blue safety flags.*

   As a further precaution, the recommendation is that the use of the color blue be restricted only for the indication of hazards on railroad territory. By not allowing other signs, labels and markings to use this color, blue takes on a special significance. A similar requirement has been imposed in the use of diamond shaped labels with respect to the transportation of hazardous materials. Containers with hazardous materials that are intended for transport may not include any other diamond shaped symbols to reduce the chance of an operator overlooking any hazardous item. Under this imposed restriction, blue signs and lights in train yards would only be allowed for blue flag protection, eliminating the possibility that an operator might use blue lights or signs for other purposes, such as indicating the movement of their trains in a complex rail yard. For example, the Columbia and Cowlitz railroad uses a blue strobe light on top of their locomotives to distinguish them from the other safety lights in the train yard (Columbia & Cowlitz, 2007). Although this may be an effective differentiation, it may reduce the effectiveness of the light as a specific blue flag to indicate that the locomotive should not be moved if it is also used as a light to identify the movement of a train among other moving vehicles.

   This restriction would also help clarify rules for other railroad industry partners who operate in train yards, but are not specifically railroad operators. For example, the military must also operate trains in different countries and be able to interpret the rules wherever they operate. The less ambiguous rules are, then the easier it will be for military personnel to safely operate around the world. In other cases, such as in loading docks, and intermodal transfer stations, many different types of transportation must interact. In these cases, clear rules of operation that nonrailroad personnel can follow will improve safety in these facilities.

8. Training – *Train all railroad employees on newly adopted blue safety flag standards and requirements.*

Railroads should also consider training employees and customers on any newly adopted blue safety flag standards. At a minimum, training should develop recognition of safety blue, as well as the physical parameters of blue safety flags and lights and warning messages. During transition periods, companies should instruct employees on the use of existing as well as new blue safety flag devices until such time as the transition is complete. Additionally, having rules about who can place equipment under blue flag protection and who can remove it will also help increase safety. The rules should clearly state who can place a device under blue flag protection, what procedures should be followed to have established blue flag protection, documentation, and the procedures to be followed when removing blue flag protection. Additional training will be required for all personnel who are eligible for placing and removing blue flag protection.

6. References

American National Standards Institute. (2007). *American National Standard: Safety Tags and Barricade Tapes (for Temporary Hazards) Z535.5*. Rosslyn, VA: National Electrical Manufacturers Association. Rosslyn, VA: National Electrical Manufacturers Association.

American National Standards Institute. (2006). *American National Standard for Safety Color Code Z535.1*. Rosslyn, VA: National Electrical Manufacturers Association.

Bogart, C.H. (2006). Blue flags: When seeing blue means "stop." *Trains Magazine*. Retrieved from: http://trains.com/trn/default.aspx?c=a&id=271.

Canadian National Railway Company. (2006). *2006 Railroad Customer's Safety Handbook*. Retrieved on February 15, 2007 from: www.cn.ca/about/safety/pdf/2006CustomerSafetyHandbook_eng.pdf.

Cardosi, K.M. (1998). *Use of Color in ATC Displays*. DOT/FAA/AR-97/ DOT-VNTSC-FAA-98-5.

Chan, K., & Lau, H. (2009). *International Review of Railway Safety Practices for the Independent Transport Safety and Reliability Regulator (ITSRR)*, Sydney, Australia: Lloyd's Register.

Chapanis, A. (1996). *Human Factors in Systems Engineering*, New York: John Wiley & Sons.

Columbia and Cowlitz. (2007, May 15). In *Wikipedia, the free encyclopedia*. Retrieved on February 15, 2007 from: http://en.wikipedia.org/wiki/Columbia_and_Cowlitz_Railway.

Coplen, M., & Lee, M.T. (2006). Canadian Pacific Railway Mechanical Service's 5-Alive Safety Program Shows Promise in Reducing Injuries. *Research Results*, U.S. Department of Transportation, Federal Railroad Administration, RR 06-14.

Dreyfuss, H. (1972). *Symbol Source Book*, New York: McGraw-Hill.

ENSCO. (2007). *Safety Manual for FRA Survey Cars Automated Track Inspection Program (ATIP)*. Pub. No. DOT-FR-05-55.

Federal Aviation Administration, 14 CFR Part 23.1397, Color specifications (2010).

Federal Highway Administration. (2006). *Manual of Uniform Traffic Control Devices for Streets and Highways*, Washington DC: U.S. Department of Transportation, Federal Highway Administration.

Federal Railroad Administration, 49 CFR 218 (2009a).

Federal Railroad Administration, 49 CFR 218 Subpart B – *Blue Signal Protection of Workers* (2009b).

Federal Railroad Administration, 49 CFR 240.121 Appendix F (2009c).

International Commission on Illumination. (1994). *Review of the Official Recommendations of the CIE for the Colours of Signal Lights (CIE 107-94)*. Vienna, Austria: International Commission on Illumination.

International Commission on Illumination. (1988). *Roadsigns (CIE 074-1988)*, Vienna, Austria: International Commission on Illumination.

International Commission on Illumination. (1983). *Recommendations for surface colours for visual signaling (CIE 39.2 83)*. Vienna, Austria: International Commission on Illumination.

International Commission on Illumination. (1975). *Colors of Light Signals (CIE 2.2 75)*. Vienna, Austria: International Commission on Illumination.

Kleffman, D.R. (1987). U.S. Patent 4,637,668, Washington, DC: U.S. Patent and Trademark Office.

Lafreniere, R.G. (2006). U.S. Patent 7,032,865, Washington, DC: U.S. Patent and Trademark Office.

Loumiet, J.R. & Jungbaer, W.G. (2005). *Train Accident Reconstruction*, Tucson AZ: Lawyers & Judges Publishing Co.

Smallman, H.S., & Boynton, R.M. (1993). On the usefulness of basic colour coding in an information display. *Displays*, *14*(3), 158-165.

Society of Automotive Engineers. (1998). General Recommendations for Colors, Aeronautical Lights and Lighting Equipment (AS25050). Warrendale, PA: Society of Automotive Engineers.

Standards Association of Australia. (1985). *Australian Standard (AS 1318-1985) Use of Colour for the Marking of Physical Hazards and the Identification of Certain Equipment in Industry: SAA Industrial Safety Colour Code*. Homebush, NSW, Australia: Standards Australia.

Transport Canada. (2001). *Railway Safety Regulations*, Canadian Transportation Accident Investigation and Safety Board Act SOR/92-446. Retrieved on February 15, 2007 from: http://www.canlii.org/ns/laws/regu/2001r.144/20071213/whole.html

United States Office of Technology Assessment. (1979). *Railroad Safety – U.S.-Canadian Comparison*, NTIS order no.: PB-301397. Library of Congress Catalog Card Number: 79-600145. Washington, DC: Office of Technology Assessment.

United States Office of Technology Assessment. (1978). *An Evaluation of Railroad Safety*, NTIS order no.: PB-281169. Library of Congress Catalog Card Number: 78-600051. Washington, DC: Office of Technology Assessment.

Wickens, C.D., & Hollands, J.G. (2000). *Engineering Psychology and Human Performance, Third Edition*. Upper Saddle River, NJ: Prentice Hall.

Appendix A.
Design and Procurement Guidelines

These guidelines are based on following the recommendations put forward in ANSI Z535.1 and ANSI Z535.5. The reader is referred to these documents for additional details. The specific recommendations have been modified to accommodate the railroad-specific use of the color blue to convey danger.

The following steps guide the reader through the necessary decisions required in designing and procuring blue safety flag devices.

Color Specification – Safety Blue is the recommended color. It has chromaticity coordinates of 0.1691, 0.1744. The Pantone ink formula for printing this color is: 13.5 parts Process Blue, and 2.5 parts Reflex Blue. The closest Pantone matching ink is 2945C. Manufacturers should be required to produce a blue safety flags that meet one of these three specifications for Safety Blue.

1. Text – The printed message on a blue flag requires several considerations:

    a. Viewing Distance – the height of the text is based on the viewing distance. Determining the safe viewing distance in feet will determine the minimum letter height needed.
        i. For ideal viewing conditions, the letter height in inches is equal to the viewing distance in feet divided by 25.
        ii. For unfavorable viewing conditions, the minimum letter height in inches is equal to the viewing distance multiplied by 0.084.

    b. Font – Sans serif fonts for all text. The text color should be white on a safety blue background.

2. Message Content – The message content should contain the following elements:

    a. The signal word should be "danger," written in all capital letters, indicating the potential of death or serious injury if the warning is not followed.

    b. An exclamation point in an equilateral triangle should be used as a safety symbol. The triangle should be white and the exclamation point printed in safety blue.

    c. The safety message should include a statement of the hazard, an action statement to avoid the hazard, and a consequence statement of what will happen if the caution is ignored.

    d. A signature block, if appropriate, can be added to provide additional details about who placed the flag, when it was placed and when it is expected to be removed.

    e. Text appropriate to the location should be used.

The examples below are offered as an illustration of potential flag layouts only and are not intended to be substituted for any specific requirements the user may have. Additional layout guidelines are available in ANSI Z535.5.

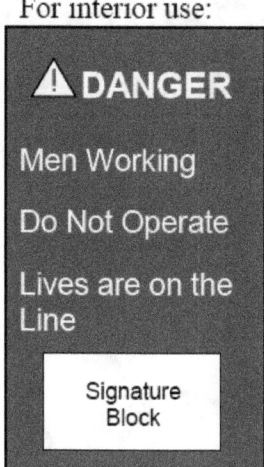

For exterior use:

⚠ DANGER

Men Working

Do Not Move

Lives are on the Line

Signature Block

For interior use:

⚠ DANGER

Men Working

Do Not Operate

Lives are on the Line

Signature Block

3. <u>Materials</u> – The materials used for safety flags depend on the specific design application. Flags intended for mounting on poles attached to rails are most often made of metal. Flags intended for use within a locomotive cab can be made of lighter weight material, such as hard rigid plastic. Durable fabrics, such as rubberized vinyl, also may be used both in exterior and interior applications.

4. <u>Mounting</u> – The method for mounting the blue flag must also be specified in the design and procurement of a blue safety flag. Poles with clamps for attaching to rails can be specified for hanging signs at specific heights above the top of the rail. Flags intended for use in the cab can be fastened to the controls using nylon tie wraps. The mounting devices should be secured and not easily dislodged when bumped or when exposed to high winds or other forces.